Country Farm Scenes
COLORING BOOK

TERESA GOODRIDGE

D1367069

DOVER PUBLICATIONS, INC.
MINEOLA, NEW YORK

A tranquil country setting is the perfect place to "Keep Calm and Farm On," as pictured in this charming coloring book. Rustic scenes include everything from birds perched on a watering can and bountiful fruit and vegetable stands to a delectable picnic lunch, a pumpkin-filled pickup truck, and a kitchen promising home-baked goods. These thirty-one realistically rendered images, specially designed for the advanced colorist, are printed on one side only and perforated for easy removal and display.

Bibliographical Note

Country Farm Scenes Coloring Book is a new work,
first published by Dover Publications, Inc., in 2019.

International Standard Book Number
ISBN-13: 978-0-486-83673-7
ISBN-10: 0-486-83673-8

Manufactured in the United States by LSC Communications
83673803   2020
www.doverpublications.com

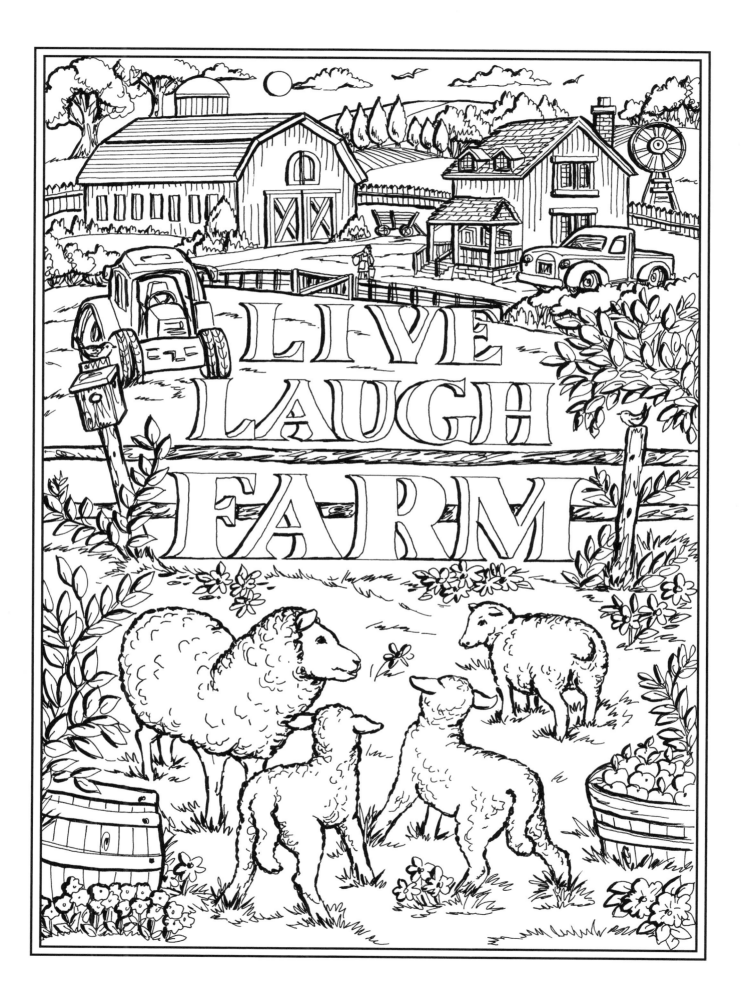

FLOWERS FOR SALE

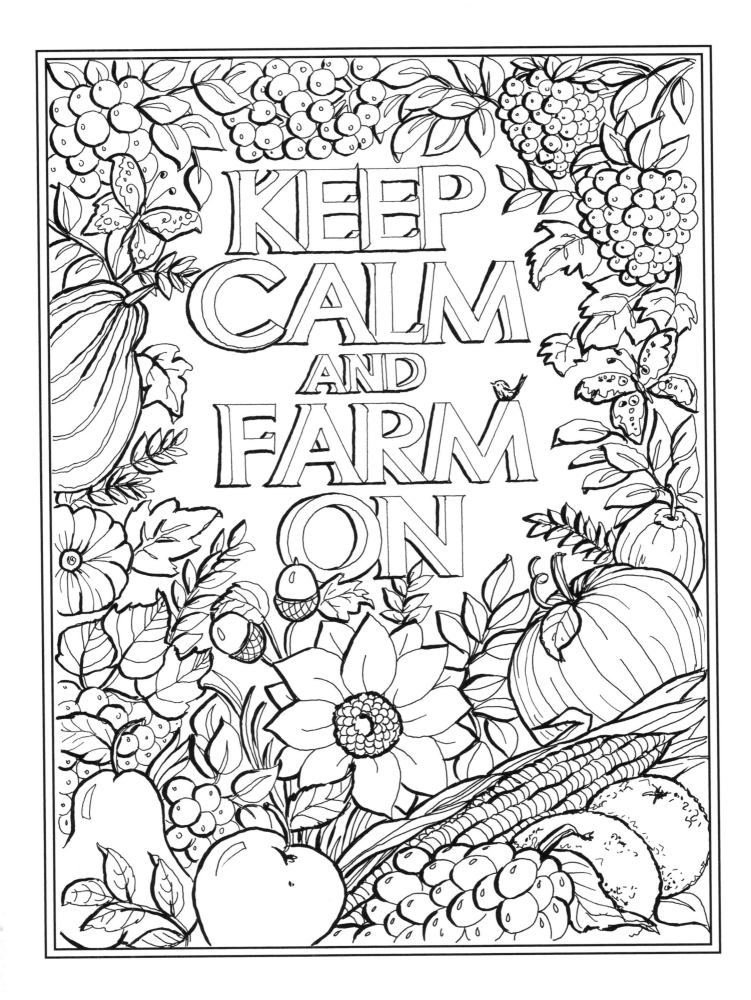

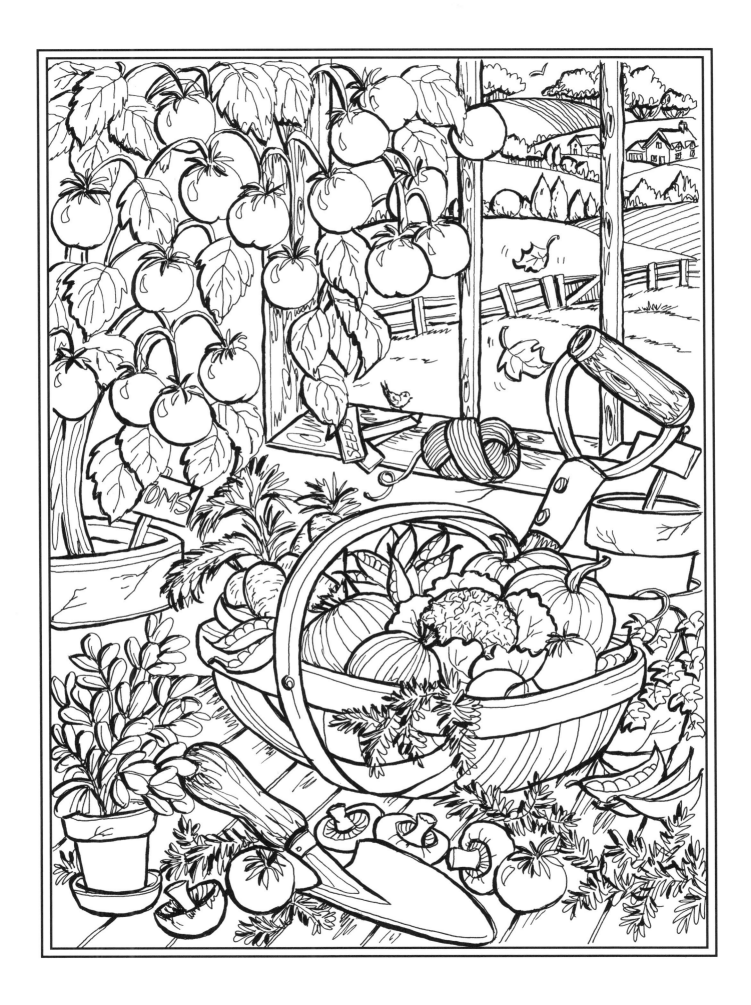